Mommy's Imaginary Friend

A Way to Talk to Young Children About Depression

Written by Jessika Allsop

Illustrated by Melissa Mae

I have a friend named Leon, but you can't see him.
Nobody but me can see him.

Leon isn't a kid like me, he is a dog.
He has a big red nose, blue floppy ears, and he is covered in spots.

Leon and I play together all the time.
He always lets me pick the games we play.

Leon even lets me be the ship's captain when we play pirates.
Leon is always nice and he makes me laugh.

My Mommy told me she has a friend no one else can see too.
His name is Marvin.

I don't think Marvin is fun or nice like Leon.
Marvin makes Mommy sad.

Only Mommy can see Marvin, but she has told me what he looks like.

Marvin is really tall, he has blue horns, a BIG nose, and very hairy feet.
Sometimes I'm glad I can't see him.

Marvin makes Mommy act different.
She doesn't smile and laugh as much when he's around.

She doesn't want to play outside or even take us to the park.
That makes Leon feel bad.

I guess Marvin really likes to watch movies.
Sometimes when he is here, Mommy and I cuddle and watch a lot of movies.

That's not too bad, Leon and I like movies.

Just like Leon, Marvin isn't always around.
Sometimes he goes to his own home, wherever that is.

I can always tell when Marvin is with Mommy.
He makes Mommy cry and then she just wants to take naps all day.

When Marvin makes Mommy cry, it makes me sad
and I give her a great big hug and yell, "Go away Marvin!"

Mommy says my hugs and cuddles help her feel warm and happy.

Mommy goes to a special doctor and he talks to her about Marvin.
The doctor teaches Mommy how to tell Marvin to go away.

Leon and I like to watch the fish while Mommy talks to the doctor.

Daddy says Marvin will go away someday and Mommy will smile and laugh more.
Hopefully then she will want to play pirates with Leon and me.

Maybe then we can go to the park because she won't need so many naps.
I hope Marvin goes away soon.

Even when Marvin is around, Mommy always remembers
to call me her bug-a-boo and tell me she loves me.
She even remembers to tell Leon she loves him too.

The Author

Jessika Allsop didn't ever plan on becoming an author, it was from her own battle with depression that she received the inspiration for "Mommy's Imaginary Friend". Jessika has a bachelor's degree in Marriage and Family Studies with an emphasis in Early Childhood Education. She is a stay-at-home-mom and currently resides in Utah with her two sons and her husband.

Learn more about Jessika and "Mommy's Imaginary Friend" at www.MommysImaginaryFriend.com

The Illustrator

Melissa Mae knew she wanted to be an artist the first time she watched Disney's "Snow White" at the age of 4. She is a full time illustrator and set designer for local films and commercials in Utah, where she lives with her husband and two kids.

Learn more about Melissa and her work at www.TheCheekyWhale.com